Girona

city guide

TRIANGLE ▼ POSTALS

Girona, an open city

There are few opportunities to discover a city as unique as this one. Erected by man to fit his needs, its splendid architectural legacy has never been able to put out the flames of its inhabitants' great vitality. Girona was born on a hill, fed by the waters of the Onyar, a short way from an ancient road that connected the two sides of the Pyrenees. It has taken shape with an enviable balance between the water that passes and the stone that endures. The omnipresent cathedral, with the alleys in its shadow leading up to it, is the head of a hierarchical aesthetic order. At its feet unfolds a paradise for lovers of art and culture.

Whoever arrives by car would do well to park it somewhere until their day of departure. Girona is a city to be enjoyed on foot and without the need to obsess oneself with the routes marked out to the millimetre that appear on some maps. There is no need to worry about getting lost in the "stone labyrinth" – as it has been called – because it is homely labyrinth that never betrays.

An absolute must is a stroll along the walls surrounding the city, today converted into a splendid raised pathway. It represents the best metaphor for change in a community that has left behind the old fears and now shows all its attractions with the utmost pride.

Girona society is often accused of having become rather bourgeois, a provincial air that it has not fully shaken off. People live well in Girona but without fuss, very much behind closed doors. Neither do they deserve their unsociable reputation. You will just need to give them a little time, approaching them carefully, so that a noble and open attitude to the visitor will eventually surface. This guide provides a compendium, very useful for the tourist in a hurry, of the city's main attractions, but it also carries tips and suggestions for those who wish to calmly discover the city's most hidden heartbeat.

Montjuïc is a privileged watchtower for enjoying the firework displays

Water and stone

Water and stone were two decisive elements in the city's formation: the first guaranteed life; the second, its monumental future. Girona is situated at the confluence of four rivers: the Ter, Güell, Galligants and, evidently, the Onyar, the shores of which form the city's backbone. Girona stone is calcareous, made up of numulites, easily manageable but hard at the same time. The material that has formed the network of alleys, steps and buildings of the old quarter were dug from the city's quarries.

Girona was originally an important capital due to its strategic position, being situated where the Via Augusta of the Roman period crossed. It became a fortress, *oppidum*, with the name of Gerunda, with a fortified precinct between the Onyar and Galligants rivers and was always a land of mixed ethnic groups.

In the second half of the 3rd century it was invaded by Franks and Germans, resulting in the movement of the walls. Christianity took hold in the Roman city between the 3rd and 4th centuries and from the 5th century onwards, it appears as the See of a Christian diocese.

After the fall of the Roman Empire, Girona fell into the hands of the Visigoths. The Muslims held power briefly until the people of Girona handed over the city to Charlemagne, who created the county of Girona, the early centre of the Marca Hispánica, subjected to the Frankish Empire.

At the end of the 12th century, the city experienced tremendous growth which forced it to extend beyond the walls, thus forming the extramural districts such as Sant Pere, Santa Maria, Mercadal and Sant Feliu.

In the year 890 there had been a well-established Jewish quarter, made up of some twenty Hebrew families. The community reached a thousand members and their presence

There is a better view of the city from the Wall path

The stone of Girona is crumbling due to the numulites

The Rambla is the display case of Girona society

remained until the expulsion of the Jews from the Iberian Peninsula, which took place in 1492. The perimeters of the walls were extended in the 14th century, even reaching as far as the left bank of the Onyar, although this barrier would advance very slowly with the passing of time.

Between the 14th and 15th centuries, Girona, with a population of 8,000 inhabitants, became one of the main cities in Catalonia. However, the ravages of the Black Death and the economic reverses suffered in the following centuries slowed down its growth. The Black Death of 1348 claimed over one thousand lives and the decline continued well into the 18th century.

A defensive bastion against French invasions, Girona suffered constant sieges, the most striking ones occurring between 1285 and 1462. It became known as the City of the Sieges after the Napoleonic sieges in 1808 and 1809, which left a deep imprint on the city's urban framework and social fabric.

Growth took place on the left bank of the Onyar in the mid 19th century, from the Barcelona road onwards. The railway reached Girona in 1862, the same time as early industrialisation was taking place.

At the beginning of the 20th century the city had fifteen thousand inhabitants, and took an active part in the cultural renovation that developed all around Catalonia.

Girona was left in a bad way after the Civil War with buildings destroyed by the Francoist air attacks and churches looted by the anti-clerics. The cruellest suffering, however, was reserved for the people: deaths, executions by firing squad, families dispersed, accusations between neighbours... it was obligatory to pass through Girona on the way to exile and the city's inhabitants watched the painful march of the defeated towards the French border. The Francoist promise

The oldest streets preserve the trade guild footprint

The colourist fluvial façade is the emblem of Girona

The chiaroscuro reigns in the alleys of the Barri Vell

The "correfoc" disturbs the urban peace

On Saturdays, the stands of the artisans occupy the Pont de Pedra

La Devesa is the city's giant lung

of "bread, justice and pardon" was mere words and brutal repression was unleashed.

By the 60s, the period of autocracy had been overcome and the dramatic economic changes boosted by neo-capitalist development took place. They were the "happy 60s", the time of the 600, a small car manufactured by SEAT. Later on, the world economic crisis of 1973 would serve as an accompaniment of the selfsame crisis of Francoism.

During the 50s and 60s, Girona received a great many emigrants from the south of the peninsula. With these recently arrived citizens the population grew to 33,000 inhabitants. In order to form the "Greater Girona", in 1963 the villages of Santa Eugènia, Sant Daniel and Palau Sacosta were annexed. Later the land of Sant Gregori, Celrà, Salt and Sarrià were also added. In a reverse of this policy, Salt and Sarrià were separated in 1983.

In 1979, the first democratic local elections were won by the PSC, the socialist party, which since then – for over twenty years now – has held municipal power. The city council has been the driving force behind the organisation and modernisation of the city. Progress has often brought with it the disappearance of some or other picturesque corner of the old quarter. It is what politicians call "fluffing up".

Since the 80s, Girona stands out as being one of the cities with the highest income per capita in Spain. It also features amongst the first places in the annual bank reports which measure the standard of living of the towns. Urban growth is unstoppable and it is foreseen that the lack of building land will make the expansion into the neighbouring localities inevitable. Greater Girona will have arrived, making it obligatory to share services. Communication systems take us into the future: the TGV (high-speed train) wants to come through.

The Baroque stairway: simple design, boundless size

The large vaulting gives a feeling of dizziness

The Plaça dels Apòstols is a very balanced monumental whole

The cathedral

The outline, in harmony with the bell tower of the church of Sant Feliu, rules over the city imposing its magnificent presence. It dominates the view of anyone arriving from the north of the city. In order to visit it, a climb up the steep, dark and narrow alleys of the old quarter is required. The Carrer de la Força, on one side, and the Sobreportes Portal on the other, leap onto the unsuspecting visitor in the square. The eyesight, accustomed to the darkness, then receives the twofold shock of the sudden light and the monumental grandiloquence of the façade.

Located at the highest point of old Girona, its scenographic impact seems to be magnified by the great **Baroque stairway** (18th century), which serves as its plinth. The whole vision makes other notable constructions alongside it shrink in comparison, such as the **Casa Pastors** (18th century) and the **Pia Almoina** (14th century), headquarters of the Architects' College. The stairway's strength derives from a combination of *seny* (good sense) and its stylistic content, with the *rauxa* (wild audacity) of its exaggerated proportions. After climbing the 90 steps, often used as an enormous grandstand for watching shows of all kinds, you have to catch your breath on the third landing, stand back and admire the sober Baroque façade (17th-18th centuries). A tableau at three levels with integrated sculptures unfolds beneath the large rose window. Its only tower, not repeated on the left, makes it quite unique. Ravaged by the storms, the bronze angel that crowns it, and which serves as a weather vane, had to be changed thirty years ago. Salvador Dalí stated that its face was sculpted onto the façade and it is not difficult to make out. The relief work on the doors deserves attention, but it is upon entering when the vertigo and dizziness of the interior space captures the visitor and makes them feel like a mere speck of dust.

It possesses the widest **Gothic style vault** in the world at nearly 23 metres. In the initial project for the cathedral, work on which began in the 14th century and continued through trials and tribulations until the 18th century, three naves were planned, but the bold idea of a single vault was finally decided upon. Fifty years of heated discussions and two consultations of prestigious architects of the time were needed before the bishop and the canons of the *Seu* (See) were convinced that the work would withstand pressure. The nave awakens passionate eulogies. The Catalan poet Joan Maragall said that on looking at such a high vault he was sure that above it there could only be the "canopy of heaven". There are many artists who consider it to be one of the most impressive spaces in the world. The powerful beams of multicoloured light that are scattered from the poly-

The capitals are a mine of fantasy and creativity

chrome stained-glass windows, created between the 14th and 16th centuries, provide the austere stone with great vitality.

The veritable Achilles Heel of this imposing cathedral is a little fossilised worm, the size of an aspirin: the **numulites**. Its calcium shell increased the stone deterioration and meant the façade had to be restored, including the changing of entire blocks, between 2000 and 2001.

The interior of the cathedral contains many artistic treasures of differing styles. Among them feature the **altar stone** of the main altar (11th century), carved in alabaster, the **Throne of Charlemagne** (11th century), in marble, and the baldaquin and altar piece of the main altar (14th century), both in silver. The face of the alabaster sculpture of **Countess Ermessenda** (14th century), by Guillem de Morell, is one of the reference works of Gothic art: her eyes, closed to the mundane world, seem to open up to the serene light of the beyond.

Romanesque cloister

The cloister, together with the **Tower of Charlemagne** (12th century), is in Lombardy style and acting as a buttress for the Gothic cathedral, are the only Romanesque constructions that have survived the mixture of styles and constructions that have made up the cathedral's history. Over the pagan temple the Romanesque church was built, and over that the Gothic version, which was in turn replaced by Baroque architecture. A saint was undressed in order to dress another. **The cloister** (12th-13th centuries) is reached from the side of the chapel of l'Esperança. It is unique in the world due to the trapezoidal form of the double colonnade and the richness of the sculptures on the capitals. The 85 supporting elements, between columns and pillars, are a

The two-tailed mermaid has given rise to myths and legends

Detail of the cathedral door

The tapestry of "The Creation" expresses the spirit of an era

The Beatus is a veritable bibliographic jewel

Arabic chest of Hixem II, an exceptional piece

feast of creativity. The biblical scenes alternate with imaginative representations of flora and fauna. Impossible beasts, the original sin, Noah constructing his Ark, the slaughter of the innocents... it is the spirit of the Middle Ages petrified in stone. The builders immortalised themselves on some of the capitals. According to the German musicologist Magnus Scheneider, the cloister possesses a hidden musical dimension. He states that the monks passed through the grounds paying attention to the animals sculpted on the capitals, which represented musical notes, giving them the score for singing the hymn "Mater Dolorosa".

Cathedral Museum

Plaça de la Catedral. Tel. 972 21 44 26. Opening times : from 10 a.m. to 2 p.m. and 5-6 p.m.; Sundays, from 10 a.m. to 2 p.m. ; closed Mondays. Price : 3 €

The **tapestry of the Creation** is the Cathedral Museum's shining star and the only piece of textile dating from the 11th-12th centuries that is still in a decent state. It was embroidered in chainstitch, with brightly coloured wool over a rough linen fabric. The weavers of this enormous baldaquin measuring 3.65 x 4.70 metres, which was to be hung behind the altar, placed the Pantocrator in the centre. From the centre outwards appear – like concentric circles, waves of life, like ripples in the water – the stages of creation, the four winds and, on the outside, the passing of the months, the seasons, the rivers and mountains of paradise.

The **Beatus** (10th century), a book of commentaries on the Book of the Apocalypse by the Beato de Liébana, illustrated with miniatures, is considered to be one of the most beautiful in the world. In its fantastic pre-Romanesque and coloured illustrations of a caliphal influence, the friar Emeterio and the nun Eude, the book's authors, clearly burnt the midnight oil in producing it. Also of interest in the museum is the small **chest of Hixem II** (10th century), one of the finest Arab chests on the Iberian peninsula; the **Virgin of the Seu** (12th century), a wooden sculpture that watched over the Romanesque cathedral; and the carefully produced bible that belonged to Charles V of France (15th century).

The explosion of symbolism in the cloister scenes and on the tapestry of the Creation form an excellent introduction to the spirit of Romanesque. Art was the vehicle for the supernatural message of which intellectualism has today disarmed of its power of suggestion. In Romanesque art the use of symbols were the direct communication with a reality that was beyond experience and naturally went, in a period of illiteracy, beyond that of the written word.

Sarcophagus of the lion hunt

Church of Sant Feliu

PUJADA DE SANT FELIU, 29. OPEN DAILY AT TIMES OF WORSHIP, FREE ENTRY.

Its stylised bell tower, a loyal sentry of Santa Maria, was blunted by a wicked streak of lightning. The sharp pinnacles, pointed with filigree befitting the Nordic style, give it a cheery air, like the lights of a festival. The **church of Sant Feliu** (14th-17th centuries) was built where an African missionary of the same name was martyred or buried. The ground plan, initially Romanesque, was finished and covered with a Gothic vault. A pretty trifoliate form that surrounds the church blends these styles together. The Gothic façade, facing west, reveals an imposing stairway, but the whole space loses strength due to the empty spaces that should house sculptures and a plinth which emphasise the fact that the twin tower is missing, an element that never went beyond the planning stage.

Worth seeing is the altar piece of the main altar (16th century), the sepulchre of Saint Narcissus, patron saint of Girona, and the reclining Christ (14th century), an alabaster work by Aloi de Montbrai, of an uncommon naturalism.

Joined to the church, the luxurious **neo-classical chapel** of Sant Narcís (18th century) is covered with marble and paintings. On the altar rests the silver sepulchre containing the relics of the patron saint of Girona. The most aesthetically stunning aspect of this visit, however, is in the eight pagan and Christian sepulchres encrusted into the presbytery walls, combining a bold design and skilful execution. It is the most interesting series in the Iberian Peninsula. Made from marble, the two oldest (2nd century) represent Proserpina kidnapped by Pluto and a lion-hunting party.

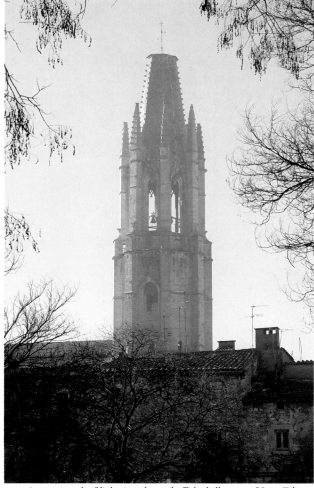

A rogue streak of lightning chopped off the bell tower of Sant Feliu

Arab baths

C/ Ferran el Catòlic, s/n. Tel. 972 21 32 62. Opening times : from 10 a.m. to 2 p.m. (weekdays and public holidays; closed on Mondays in winter). In summer it is also open from 4-7 p.m. Price : 1.50 €

The people of Girona in the Middle Ages could not have found a better way of glorifying the bath than with this temple of light. The **Arab baths** of Girona (12th-13th centuries) are the best-preserved public baths in Catalonia. Despite their name, their origins are not in the Arab period, but are Romanesque, but were built following the spa structure popularised so much by the Muslims, in turn copied from the constructive model of the ancient Roman thermal baths. The building preserves all the elements common to public baths and evokes the warm atmosphere of relaxation and escape. The east entrance leads to the changing room, a space for chatting and mixing. In the centre is an octagonal pool surrounded by slender Romanesque columns with Corinthian capitals. These columns support an octagonal tambour with a skylight to let in the sun's rays, lighting up the space and giving it great strength.

The *frigidarium* is a large hall of cold baths with stone vaulting and latrines. The *caldarium* was for enjoying a comforting hot bath, whereas the *tepidarium* was the room for warm steam baths and massages. A fully integrated hot water system, which came from an area with a heater, boilers and cisterns, emptied the water through the drains and guaranteed the perfect functioning of this bathhouse. It ceased operating in the 16th century. In 1929 it passed into public ownership and was restored by the leading architects Rafael Masó and Emili Blanc.

The lantern of the Arab Baths lights up the interior

Points of interest

Sant Pere de Galligants, monastery and archeological museum

C/ SANTA LLÚCIA, 1. TEL. 972 20 26 32. OPENING TIMES: FROM 10 A.M. TO 1.30 P.M. AND 4-7 P.M.; SUNDAYS AND PUBLIC HOLIDAYS, FROM 10 A.M. TO 2 P.M.; CLOSED ON MONDAYS. PRICE: 1.80 €

The **monastery of Sant Pere de Galligants**, an old Benedictine abbey, and the church of Sant Nicolau, both from the 12th century, form an elegant Romanesque monument situated on the right bank of the River Galligants, in Carrer de Santa Llúcia. Sant Pere de Galligants is noted for the rose window that dominates the church's sober façade, as well as the bell tower, with three floors, the lower one being square and the other two octagonal. The smallish cloister creates an intimate space with fine examples of Romanesque sculpture that reproduce scenes from the New Testament. The capitals, many of them adorned with characters from Christ's childhood and with plant and animal iconography, are in the same style and period as those in the cathedral. The ground plan is basilican and the current church of Sant Pere de Galligants consists of three naves and a cross-aisle, with four apses, and was built in 1130.

The items to be found in the **Archaeological Museum** provide clues to the history of mankind from his appearance in the territory, during the Middle Palaeolithic era, through to the beginnings of the medieval period. The collections, taken from excavations close to the city, occupy the side naves and the apse aisles. The Romanisation is one of the best-represented periods. Among the items that really must be seen feature the trousseaus from Neolithic sepulchres, the lead plaque with Iberic writing from the Castell de la Fosca, the Iberian and Greek tombstones from Empúries, the antenna sword from Camallera and the series of objects from daily Roman life. Also of interest is the Roman sepulchre "of the seasons", from Empúries and exhibited in the old vestry.

Situated opposite Sant Pere de Galligants, the **chapel of Sant Nicolau** could be defined, due to its size, as a pocket-sized church. It is a balanced and quite beautiful building, despite the exaggerated mark left in it by the restoration work. The current church is a 12th century building, but there are vestiges of a previous construction in its basement. Due to the expulsion of the monastery by the church authorities, Sant Nicolau was left abandoned, and until it was purchased by the council, which restored it after 1940, it was used as a leather warehouse. The building presently houses the occasional art exhibition, mainly of contemporary work.

Sant Pere de Galligants emerges from the gardens

The capitals show animal and plant iconography

Side view of the chapel of Sant Nicolau

Points of interest

La Rambla

This is the privileged display case for the vices and virtues of local society. There are few places where the city's heartbeat throbs with such energy. The local people use the verb *"ramblejar"* for their comings and goings along this lively artery, practising the art of seeing and being seen. La Rambla is an unavoidable debating centre, and anyone in a hurry always runs the risk of being trapped by a *"romeguera"*, the name given here to the irrepressible charlatans, always ready for a long conversation. On the terraces of the bars, the midday vermouth drinkers chase the occasional glimpses of sun in winter, and in summer, the cool air beneath the splendid vaulted arches. Trading has gone on here since medieval times, when there was a market there. On Saturday mornings the flower stalls spread their colours and perfumes.

The **Rambla de la Llibertat** runs parallel to the River Onyar and leads the passer-by to the feet of the old and monumental Girona. The view of the cathedral from here is unsurpassable, closed in by remnants of sky that frame the façades and rooftops. Going up the Rambla, alongside the building that houses the **Tourist Office** and the **City Exhibition Rooms**, is the monument in memory of the journalist and writer **Carles Rahola**, executed by Francoist troops in 1939. Going down, on the left-hand side, projects the Modernist façade of **Can Norat** (1912). The route should be repeated, this time along the low and shady arcades, being careful not to bump your head on the stone, a regular occurrence if you walk too close to the columns. A pleasant surprise here is the detailed map of Paris painted on one of the ceilings. It was painted in the last century at the behest of a shop that kept its eye on what was happening in French fashion.

The Rambla is a hive of activity on specific days

The flower stands perfume and colour Saturdays

The shade of the arcade and the shop windows attract pedestrians

The Fontana d'Or is an imposing Gothic palace

Pujada de Sant Domènec, one of the most beautiful spaces in the city

Pujada de Sant Domènec and Fontana d'Or

The crossing stairways known as **Pujada** (climb) **de Sant Domènec**, a calvary of watercolour painters and photographers, forms one of the most beautiful and balanced corners of the old quarter. The steps on the right lead to the dramatic façade of the **church of Sant Martí** (16th-18th centuries) and the left-hand stairs pass below the lowered arches of the **Casa dels Agullana** (16th and 17th centuries), an elegant architectural solution linking the two houses of the family.

A leading example of the old stately homes can be found in the **Fontana d'Or** (13th-16th centuries), an enormous Gothic palace built over Romanesque porches. The large main room has slender carved stone capitals. The central courtyard, with stairway and raised gallery, is one of the few interior gardens open to the public.

The museum displays stone tombstones

Bonastruc ça Porta - Jewish Museum

CARRER DE LA FORÇA, 8. TEL. 972 21 67 61. WINTER OPEN-
ING: WEEKDAYS, FROM 10 A.M. TO 6 P.M. (CLOSED ON
MONDAYS); SUMMER OPENING: OPEN UNTIL 8 P.M. AND ON
PUBLIC HOLIDAYS UNTIL 3 P.M. PRICE : 2 €

The **Bonastruc ça Porta centre**, site of the synagogue in
the Jewish quarter, has become the reference point for pre-
serving the essence of the Jewish legacy in the city. It is also
known by the name of the master of the Girona cabalists,
Isaac the Blind. In its reformed premises, with peaceful and
secluded courtyards, are situated the **Nahmànides Study
Institute**, the source of the historical study of the community, and the Jewish History Museum, focused on showing the
essential traits of their 500 years of history in Girona.

When Josep Pla wrote, "within the human mosaic of this
country, the most vivid tile is the Hebrew one", he was referring,
above all other considerations, to the cultural heritage. The
tombstones on show in the museum form one of the rare phys-
ical testimonies of the Jews in Girona. It is the most important
archaeological and epigraphic collection in the whole of Spain.
It was discovered at the end of the 19th century close to the
mountain of Montjuïc – mountain of the Jews –, also known as
Bou d'Or, where their cemetery was located. Dated between the
12th and 15th centuries, their inscriptions include eulogies to the
deceased and biblical quotations: "Devout, full of wisdom and
fearful of God, obeying the rule of the Lord. He died on the day
of crimes, his soul clean of sin". The Hebrew libraries were
destroyed. The fragments of manuscripts that still exist were
saved thanks to the fact that they were reused as padding for
binding old books by the municipal or ecclesiastical authorities.

The study centre preserves documents from the **Cábala**
(Tradition), a series of esoteric and theosophical teachings prac-
tised by mystical Jews in western Christian communities. Its rep-
resentative in Girona, Mossé ben Nahman, also known as Nah-
mánides or Bonastruc ça Porta, was an erudite in the matter.

The rehabilitation combines tradition and modern design

The inner courtyard is the cosiest spot of the property

The houses over the Onyar

Like the ugly duckling that transformed into a swan, the picturesque houses alongside the river were born without charm. They were built at the end of the Middle ages, facing the street that runs parallel to the **Onyar** and the backs were attached to the walls that still enveloped the old quarter. Rather than a bright urban symbol, they were then a solid containing wall and impenetrable defence. The disappearance of external enemies meant that Girona no longer turned its back on the river. Small openings began to appear in the wall, slowly but surely, and with the passing of time, these openings became the current conglomeration of windows, galleries, balconies, blinds and rooftops. The setting is always changing with the unplanned touches of colour of clothes hanging out to dry. It is, at the end of the day, a constructive disaster that has managed to achieve harmony.

The moving reflection in the waters of the Onyar round off this bright and colourful spectacle... when the limited flow permits, that is. The complacency with which the city looks at itself in this mirror leads one to suspect the Saint Narcissus, patron saint of Girona, could also have been the mythological Narcissus, in love with his own image. After its architectural rehabilitation, with Italian-style traits, started in 1983 and directed by the architects Josep Fuses and Joan M. Viader, and a treatment of colour under the direction of the Girona painters Jaume Faixó and Enric Ansesa, the river-facing façade of the city has become an indisputable postcard-metaphor of the vital Girona arising from the mediocrity of Francoism. The houses seen from the **Pont de Pedret** or the **Pont de Sant Agustí** are what clearly dominate here. This image, added to the architectural and cultural richness, is what has produced the definition of the "Catalan Florence", as some people have described Girona.

The river-facing façade is a harmonious hotch-patch of buildings

Reflections in the river. A metaphor of the water and stone

The bridges connect the old Girona with the growth areas

Bridges and floods

The river crosses the city but it does not divide it. The bridges are connecting points that enable one to overcome what is little more than a domestic obstacle. The **Pont de Pedra**, or of Isabel II (1850-56), is the biggest construction of the dozen bridges that connect the two parts of the city over the Onyar. Its sober structure of Girona calcareous stone forms three lowered arches supported by two solid cutwaters, capable of withstanding the battering of the most violent flows of water. Despite the abundance of stone, its image is very stylised and elegant.

The framework of red ironwork of the **Pont de les Peixateries Velles** (old fishmongers) built by the Gustave Eiffel company in 1876 forms another iconographic reference point of the city. Its wooden beams form the crossing for pedestrians.

The boldest construction over the River Onyar is the "platform", the name that has lasted in popular language. It was opened in 1967, officially named **Plaça de Catalunya**, with the pretentious aim of reordering the flow of traffic in the city centre. The last bridge over the Onyar before it flows into the Ter is the **Pont de Pedret**.

On days of persistent rain, the elderly citizens of Girona watch the flow of the river with great care. The Onyar has been capable on many occasions of breaking its peaceful flow, allowing the raging waters to overflow and treacherously flood the city. The floods of 1940, 1943, 1944, 1948, 1962, 1963, and 1970, among others, all bear witness to this fact. Some establishments in the district, such as the Granja Mora, preserve a visible reminder of the flood level. Contemporary architectural solutions have been able to calm the effects of the flooding, among which it is easy to make out schools of fat and lazy carp fish.

The Pont de les Peixateries Velles forms part of the Girona landscape

Points of interest

The Pont de Pedra combines solidity with stylisation

It is an excellent viewing point of the houses on the Onyar

Points of interest

The tradesman's mark

The professional guilds of artisans once marked the pulse of the city, boosting its economic and urban development. The streets, and even the districts in some cases, such as **Pedret**, for the quarrymen (*pedra* means stone), were given the name of the main activity. The streets called **Ciutadans** (citizens), **Mercaders** (merchants), **Ferreries Velles** (old iron-works), **Peixateries Velles** (old fishmongers), **Ballesteries** (crossbowmen), and many others in the vicinity make up a route of guilds and trades that we advise any visitor to keenly follow up. The route could start in the **Plaça del Vi**, an old wine market. Here is where the **Town Hall** is situated and, hidden in a corner of its inner courtyard and unseen is the **Teatre Municipal**, built in the mid 19th century Italian style with a horseshoe-shaped ground plan. The arcades of this square have solid columns which, according to the writer Josep Pla, fit the curve of the back perfectly, making up the best possible image of a clement and hospitable land.

The square leads to the street **Ciutadans**, in olden times the straightest, narrowest and most noble of the city, boxed between stately mansions in which the delicious provincial life took place. The street housed shops with carpenters, tailors and scribes, among others. The dense concentration of city trade began in this street and the Rambla. Vestiges of this past can still be found today, even in the modern shops. One should also take a stroll in the **Plaça de les Castanyes** (chestnuts) and the **Plaça dels Raïms** (grapes), which some consider to be the smallest square in the world. The mythomaniac can approach **Carrer del Sac** (sack), where a Hollywood-style star commemorates the birth of Xavier Cugat (Girona 1900-Barcelona 1990), the skilful musician who "did the Americas" and appeared in many films, leading his orchestra.

The food shops provide light and colour to the Barri Vell

Traffic is restricted in many streets

There are peaceful terraces in the colonnades of the Plaça del Vi

In the Plaça de la Independència one can dine beneath the arcades

The "Plaça de Sant Agustí" is the most rational of the city

Carrer de Santa Clara is ideal for quietly strolling

Plaça Independència and Mercadal district

In order to expand, the city had to cross the river. The **Plaça de la Independència** and the district of **Mercadal** form the first sector of expansion. Planned in 1855, the Plaça de la Independència is the square with most character in the city centre. Despite the monument dedicated to the defenders of Girona during the French siege of 1809, the citizens insist on calling it the Plaça de Sant Agustí, in memory of the convent of Augustine monks who occupied this space before the seizure of ecclesiastical assets. It was also called the **Plaça dels Cines**, because it was here where the first exhibition halls in the city were opened. With its neo-classical spirit, it was the first step taken in modern urban planning to overcome the confused and labyrinthine inheritance of the old quarter. The shadows of its stylised arcades are an invitation to sit down at the terraces of the bars and restaurants.

Carrer de Santa Clara, parallel to the river and **Carrer Nou**, which goes deep into the new Girona, are nearby spaces open to trade and strolling. The Mercadal district was the first industrial centre of the city. Later on, the sites abandoned by the factories were urbanised without planning. In the 90s, the **Plaça de la Constitució** absorbed the area, adding a grove and concrete public spaces.

Devesa Park

Its 2,500 plane trees are an artist's palette that reflects the seasonal changes. There is no better autumn postcard image than their bare branches over a carpet of dry leaves. Situated on the Ter, Onyar and Güell rivers, to the north-east of the city centre, Devesa Park is, with its 40 hectares, the most extensive city park in Catalonia. Even though the ordered plantation has been popularly attributed to the Napoleonic domination, the truth is that it was started much later, in 1859. There is, however, evidence showing that it was used as a path from the 18th century onwards.

The plantation's denseness forces the trees to grow tall. Some are over 50 metres high. Their branches form imposing vaulting of vegetation with which nature manages to emulate the cathedral nave. There is a pretty garden in the park, open during the day, surrounded by an unkempt stream. **Devesa Park** has overcome diverse obstacles in its time: diseased trees, isolation due to the surrounding roads, a crisis in users during the years when utility vehicles were so popular, but the practise of sports, the fairs and the lively night-life beneath the summer marquees are signs of vitality, not to mention the burst of life during the early morning market on Tuesdays and Saturdays.

The central path of the Devesa runs parallel to the road

The city park constitutes a peaceful isle of vegetation

There are also children's playgrounds in the park gardens

15ᵗʰ century Virgin, a Catalan piece

Contemporary art co-exists alongside Romanesque and Gothic work

Art Museum

Pujada de la Catedral, 12. Tel. 972 20 38 34. Opening times: from 10 a.m. to 7 p.m. (closed on Mondays); it closes at 6 p.m. between October and February. Also open Sundays and public holidays between 10 a.m. and 2 p.m. Price : 2 €

With its richness and coherence, and with pieces of such overwhelming beauty, the **Art Museum** shows us the artistic development that has taken place in the counties of Girona from the Visigoth era until the present. Although there is no permanent contemporary art exhibition, the tower often houses temporary exhibitions by leading modern artists. The contrast between new and old art is one of the singular hallmarks of the centre. Of special interest in Romanesque art is the **mobile altar** from Sant Pere de Rodes (10th century), in embossed silver, and the **Biga de Cruïlles**, polychrome wood dating from the 12th-13th centuries, on which a procession of monks is portrayed. The glazier's table from the cathedral (16t century) is the only surviving piece of its kind in Europe. Thanks to this worktop, the procedures followed by the imaginative glaziers of Gothic work has been revealed. The soldering of coloured glass on this very table and the use of lead formed the critical stage of his work. The **Martyrology**, a miniaturised codex, dated around 1400 and which came from the workshops of Wenceslas IV of Bohemia, contains a surprising colourist range over a gold background.

The museum possesses two exceptional pieces that deserve special attention. The **altarpiece of Sant Miquel de Cruïlles**, by Lluís Borrassà, highlighted by the colour work, and the **altarpiece of Púbol**, work of Bernat Martorell, outstanding for its composition and treatment of the human figure. Martorell introduced elements of modernity into religious painting. He was also a master in the treatment of light, with effects that are abundantly present in his pictures.

In the section given over to 20th century painting there are works by Catalan artists. Among them feature **Joaquim Vayreda**, renowned landscape artist from the Olot school, and **Santiago Rusiñol**, who broke with the earlier anecdotal realism. Although some works are given special value, the visitor can feel the seduction of art through the rich displays of furniture, ceramics, glass, silverwork and religious objects held by the museum.

Neither does the museum's contents outweigh our evaluation of the container. The **Palau Episcopal**, built in different stages during the 12th and 16th centuries, is a quite splendid building. This is shown by the façade in the Plaça dels Apòstols, the prison tower, the throne room, the large windows and the Romanesque arcades.

The pharmacy has been preserved intact

Collection of apothecary knives

Pharmacy of Santa Caterina

PLAÇA DE L'HOSPITAL, 1. TEL. 972 20 38 34 (MUSEUM OF ART).
OPEN SATURDAYS BETWEEN 10 A.M. TO 2 P.M. FREE ENTRY.

Situated on the inside of the Hospital de Santa Caterina, still fully active, its pharmacy dates from the early 18th century and preserves the most notable collection of apothecary instruments in the Catalan-speaking region. The area was restored between 1830 and 1847 and enables us to get an idea of how the old pharmacies worked. In the stately rooms one can see a great variety of beautiful pots, medicines and boxes for herbs, weights and measures. There are 300 perfectly preserved pieces in all. Moreover, attention should be paid to the Baroque paintings in the vaulted ceiling.

The **Hospital de Santa Caterina** (17th century) has a pretty central courtyard, with a large stairway, which leads to the other rooms. The building has been subjected to many reforms and extensions over the years.

Opposite the Hospital is the **Casa de Cultura**, an old hospice with a closed square ground plan (18th century) and with inner courtyards. The chapel was turned into an auditorium. It houses the city's public library and provides different cultural facilities, among which is an exhibition room.

Detail of Roman mosaic in Can Pau Birol

The first angel of the cathedral is kept in the museum

Museum of the History of the City

C/ DE LA FORÇA, 12. TEL. 972 22 22 29. OPENING TIMES :
FROM 10 A.M. TO 2 P.M. AND 5-7 P.M.(CLOSED MONDAYS);
SUNDAYS AND PUBLIC HOLIDAYS, FROM 10 A.M. TO 2 P.M.
PRIX : 2 €

A historical synthesis of the city, perfectly designed, interestingly presented and illustrated with valuable archaeological remains and artistic pieces of great quality. The route starts in the times of the first settlers to the area, with the prehistoric discoveries of Puig d'en Roca, and takes the visitor through to certain aspects of contemporary culture.

Among the material on display in the first rooms – a configuration of the Roman city – features the museums star turn: the **Roman mosaic of Can Pau Birol**. The spectacular piece, made from stone, marble, ceramic and glass paste, represents a chariot race in Circus Maximus of Rome. Watching the exciting and realistic scenes of the mosaic, the spectator is transported to a scene from the film Ben-Hur, despite the fact that this a piece of work dated 300 AD. Another historical episode recorded by the museum is the **War with France** (1808-1814), with the siege of Girona by the Napoleonic troops. The bloody resistance of the city is explained but by avoiding the heroic and grandiloquent tones given to it by the Francoist historians.

The museum examines the technological changes of the late 20th century. The evolution of printing, machinery and electrification are all well covered themes. It should be pointed out that Girona was the first city on the Iberian Peninsula to have electric street lighting, in 1886. The building preserves a sordid and disturbing redoubt, inherited from the monastic community that once occupied the church and cloister. It is a series of **vertical niches** where bodies were placed – after drying them, seated on wooden benches with holes drilled in them – apparently being the custom in the Capuchine Order. The **Baroque room** houses the two historical pieces of the city's cathedral: the old watch machinery and the bronze angel that worked as a weather vane. The **Modernism** and **Noucentisme** room has works by the Girona sculptors **Ricard Guinó** and **Fidel Aguilar**, the renowned creator of serene and exquisite figures who died at the peak of his creative youth. The route includes a space devoted to the *sardana* dance as well as having a curious collection of lead toy soldiers on display.

The museum runs an annexed hall for temporary exhibitions with a direct entrance in the Placeta de l'Institut Vell, at the very end of Carrer de la Força.

A simulated projection of the magic lantern

Reproduction of an old projection room

The cinema museum

C/ DE LA SÈQUIA, 1. E-MAIL : MUSEU CINEMA@AJGIRONA.ORG
TEL. 972 41 27 77. OPENING TIMES, MAY TO SEPTEMBER :
FROM 10 A.M. TO 8 P.M. (CLOSED ON MONDAYS) ; OCTOBER TO
APRIL : FROM 10 A.M. TO 2 P.M. TUESDAY TO FRIDAY; FROM 10
A.M. TO 8 P.M. SATURDAYS, AND 11 A.M. TO 3 P.M. SUNDAYS.
PRICES: 3 €, CONCESSIONARY ENTRANCE 1.50 €, ENTRY FOR
UNDER-16ˢ FREE.

The **Cinema Museum** of Girona was the result of some-one's fascination: the fascination felt by a bright pipsqueak, captivated before the showing of a travelling cinema in a village square. The passion for moving images did not leave him in adult life, but in fact he was fed by a new hobby: collecting. **Tomàs Mallol i Deulofeu** (Sant Pere Pescador, 1923) began collecting amateur cinema apparatus at the end of the sixties, but his inquiries soon led him towards so-called "cinema archaeology". In other words, the period in which science, technology, genius, and even sometimes chance, gave shape to the apparatus that reproduced – with effort but with increasing accuracy – reality in movement.

Cinema was officially born on the 28th of December 1895, the day in which the Lumière brothers gave the first paying public film show in a local stable, in Paris. This, however, was merely the happy birth of an invention that had been gestating for over five hundred years, and whose paternity was widely shared. The Cinema Museum explains many of the incidents that occurred during these 500 years.

The collection of lantern slides is fascinating

A technical prodigy: the Lumière camera-projector

Poster announcing the first cinema projections

The trip round the museum, which has 2,500 m² of space, starts on the third floor, where there are figures and apparatus of Chinese shadows, the most remote origin of image projection. The section devoted to **magic lanterns**, very popular instruments during the 18th and 19th centuries, is one of the museum's most suggestive. The hand-painted glass plates, some of them staggeringly detailed, were projected in the dark over a flat surface. Later came the apparatus with weird-sounding names – zootrope, praxinoscope, phenakistiscope, etc. – which were able to reconstruct movement by means of consecutive still images.

The miracle was possible thanks to the persistence of the human retina, which allows an image to remain on the retina for a fraction of a second. Advances in the field of chemistry applied to photography managed to hold reality and replace the painter. All that was missing was for movement and the photographic image to find each other. It was the Lumière brothers who were the first to make this miracle come true, and they commercialised it. Their apparatus, one of which is on show at the museum, was for filming, making copies and projecting.

The great inconvenience of winding on the film, which had frustrated earlier inventions, was solved by imitating the system used in sewing machines, which allow the material to slip off while holding it a moment so that the needle may enter. Using the same procedure, the images were stopped before a shutter and vibrations were avoided. Cinema had been born. The museum houses around 8,000 objects, apparatus and pre-cinema accessories and from the early days of cinema. It also has 15,000 documents – photographs, posters, engravings, paintings... – 800 films and a library with 700 books and magazines. It is not, however, just a simple museum with display cases: the audio-visual aids, the reproductions of machines and the interactive tools that the visitor can operate achieve the commendable aim of instructing and delighting at the same time.

Old soldier's steps have been opened up to the pedestrians

The last section of the wall leads to beautiful gardens

The wall path

The solid walls that, centuries before, surrounded and protected Girona from its enemies has become a spectacular vantage point over the city. The upper path that crowns a large stretch of the eastern sector of the wall follows a route that was once reserved for soldiers. This path, open during the day, gives the visitor an excellent feel of the city. It can be started at the bottom, in the **Jardí de la Infància**, next to the River Onyar. Very nearby, on certain days, the air-raid shelter where the people of Girona protected themselves from the bombing in the Civil War can be visited. You have to climb the towers to get an idyllic bird's-eye view.

It would be advisable to unfold the map that accompanies this guide in order to identify the symphony of architectural spaces and green spaces we can make out below us (there are also some inexcusable urban disasters). The more curious may wish to see, now without impediments, the magnificent courtyards and gardens hiding many stately homes in the steeply inclined Barri Vell (old quarter).

In the watchtower of Sant Domènec, the highest on the route, one can stop off to descend and visit the splendid historical monuments of **Sant Domènec**. The convent, of which only the façade remains, hosts classrooms of the University of Girona, which has over 10,000 students, while the church (14th century) is a splendid Gothic building with a very high nave, today awaiting restoration. The cloister (17th century) is also remarkable.

A stretch of the wall in this section provides a view of the successive additions given to it: the irregular blocks of the Roman era (1st century), the towers of the Middle Ages and the brickwork of the contemporary restoration.

The walls show the material used in each era

The university students' route crosses the Barri Vell

The city centre conceals some beautiful terraces

Daily life slows down in the pedestrian streets

The old Quarter

Situated on a hill on the right bank of the Onyar, the **Barri Vell** is an architectural *in crescendo* that culminates in its highest part with the magnificence of the cathedral. The Jewish **Call** district is the veritable heart of this privileged historic centre, which concentrates important artistic works into a reduced space. The route around the area must be taken on foot because driving through the old quarter – with narrow alleys and a great many tourists – is restricted as from its most usual entrance point, the Plaça de Catalunya. **Carrer de la Força** is the backbone of the urban labyrinth and the starting point for many visits. It was an ancient communication route with Europe that the Romans converted into Via Augusta. In other periods it served as the main street, even giving its name to the whole old centre, and there are some interesting bourgeois mansions to be seen.

The climb up to the cathedral can also be made by taking the **Escales** (steps) **de la Pera**. They start from the contemporary sculpture by Josep Maria Subirachs dedicated to the constructors of the See and end at the foot of a giant stone tank with a pretty fountain. The name comes from a Baroque Virgin attached to the wall.

The **Plaça dels Apòstols**, the old cemetery, gives access to the cathedral from the side façade. The doorway is Gothic with a lot of filigree, impressive despite the fact that the apostles are not in the spaces made for them. Among the spots that have remained immutable to the passing of time is the **Carrer dels Alemanys**, parallel to the city wall, in which German troops were billeted. The Barri Vell degenerated, but with democracy came its recovery. Today there are many rehabilitative works going on and even the "barri xino" or red light district, with shabby brothels, was demolished in 2000 to make way for the **Plaza del Pou Rodó**. The grateful visitor may seal a pact of loyalty with Girona by climbing up a column and kissing the stone **Cul de la Lleona** (the lioness's bottom) which is near the church of Sant Feliu. This ritual guarantees the visitor's return to the city.

On the steps of La Pera there is a sculpture by Subirachs

The Jewish Quarter (el Call)

The Jewish influence, the evocation of their ethereal presence, comes back to life as the **Call** is entered by its steep, shady and damp alleys. Stone labyrinths that have been able to resist the ravages of time. Sheltered by the high walls, the attentive visitors will sense the echoes of the past and allow their imagination to run free. They may be surprised at a corner by the cheerful chatting between Hebrews and Christians; further on, they will hear the screams of the terrified Jews fleeing from the stoning which they were traditionally subjected to by intolerant gentiles during Holy Week. Though still under royal protection, tensions rose as from 1391, when the community had some 800 inhabitants. The practise of money lending, which signified debts for the Christian sector, and the closeness of the Call to the cathedral and its clerics, were a permanent source of conflicts. The Jews dressed like Christians and spoke Catalan, but even so, they had to convert or leave.

The word Call, the origin of which means narrow and sunken or flooded pass, became the definition of the urban area inhabited by the Jewish population. The **Aljama** was the judicial body that ruled their economic, cultural and religious life. The heart of the Jewish quarter is the **Bonastruc ça Porta centre** (Jewish Museum). The area was defined by the Plaça de la Catedral, Carrer de la Força, the Lluís Batlle crossing and Carrer de la Claveria. Some of the old public courtyards and alleys have ended up forming part of private estates. The best route to take is to go along the little street of **Sant Llorenç** or **Carrer Cúndaro**. On the stones of the entrances to the houses in the Call, one can still see the space where the Jews placed the **mezuza**, the parchment containing religious passages.

Carrer Cundaro, in the Jewish Call

A street leading to the entrance of Isaac el Cec

The inner courtyards possess a beauty reserved only for the visitors

Peaceful gardens on the banks of the Ter

La Devesa is a paradise for sports lovers

The Devesa and the banks of the Ter

For the walker looking for peace and quiet, for the ardent sports enthusiast or for the amateur naturalist, these are two paradises of vegetation. The itinerary from the **Devesa** starts from the Caseta de la Devesa, a small building at the entrance of the gardens where the visitor can get information about nature routes and trips. It is well worth entering the gardens to see the fountain and the peacock cage; on returning we will have all our senses tuned in to capture all the nuances of the symphony of plant life awaiting us. Retaking the main avenue, with the highest trees in Catalonia, on the right hand side appears the stone platform where, many years ago, a military band marked the beat of the Girona public on their Sunday strolls. Further on is the **Camp de Mart** lawn, named after the Roman God of war (Mars) because there used to be drills for soldiers held here. It now houses the municipal sports facilities. Alongside the river are benches for picnics and a signposted path for runners.

On the banks of the Ter the city has another natural reserve, **Ribes del Ter**, ideal for birdwatching. The isle of Ter, where the river meets the Onyar, has become a protected site for wildlife. As well as gulls and sparrowhawks, ducks, herons and storks nest there.

Archaeological walk and the Sant Daniel valley

Leafy gardens, architecture, remarkable views over historic Girona and corners of unsuspecting beauty are some of the delights on offer to the visitor in the **Passeig Arqueològic.** Built between 1959 and 1961, it has contributed to re-evaluating the vestiges of the old Girona, but is criticised for breaking the surrounding architectural landscape. This green paradise is scattered between the basin of the River Galligants and a large stretch of wall from the **medieval towers of Julia and Cornelia** arise (14th century). Below the latter, in 1972 the sculptor Josep Bosch "Piculives" placed the **"housekeeper of Saint Narcissus"**, a legendary figure who prepared exquisite meals for the bishop Narciso.

Among the beautiful corners of the **Jardins dels Alemanys** (the Germans' gardens) the **portal of Queen Joana** stands out (13th century). The **Jardins de la Francesa** (the gardens of the Frenchwoman), known by this name due to the nationality of its old owner, are flanked by a stretch of wall that provides magnificent views across the city. Also close to here are the **John Lennon gardens**. From these gardens we have to climb a stretch of wall towards the Montjuïc mountain, crowned by the remains of a castle which successfully repelled invaders.

The **Vall de Sant Daniel** is an idyllic spot where crystalline springs emerge. It has an unmistakable silhouette, immortalised by painters and writers. One should visit the **Font del Bisbe** (Bishop's spring), where many of Girona's people fill up their large water bottles. In the heart of this valley, trenched by the variant of Girona, is the monastery of Sant Daniel, with a Greek cross ground plan (11th and 12th centuries) and rectangular cloister (13th century).

Garden "of the Germans", close to the Reina Joana Portal

A group of students drawing at the foot of "La Majordoma"

A green area connects the cathedral with Sant Daniel

Architect Masó

One of the leading representatives of Catalan Noucentista (nineteenth century style) architecture, Rafael Masó, left his mark on Girona with the only early 20th century buildings that are worth visiting. Schooled in Modernism, Masó was very soon attracted by the meticulous and refined architecture of Noucentisme and, after studying in Barcelona, settled in his home town of Girona, where he surrounded himself with a large group of collaborators specialised in the most diverse disciplines of applied arts: carpenters, locksmiths, quarrymen, iron workers, glaziers...

A journey through Masó's Noucentista architecture could start off in the **Farmàcia Masó Puig** (today the Farmàcia Seguer, in Carrer Argenteria), his first architectural piece in Girona. His personal and refined style combined with his boldness won only incomprehension from Girona society for Masó, allowing for part of his work to suffer from abandonment over the years. An example of this neglect would be the **Farinera** (flour factory) **Teixidor**, finally recovered as the headquarters for the El Punt newspaper. A combination of volumes and pinnacles, with white vitrified ceramic, evoke the mountains of flour in a splendid building that housed the factory, warehouses and private home. Worth noting in the Casa Masó, the architect's own home, is the façade facing

La Farinera has been the object of a perfect restoration project

Masó intervened in his birthplace

The architect designed the current Saguer pharmacy

the river, with the characteristic galleries and the popular ceramic adornments.

Near to the Farinera Teixidor is the **Casa de la Punxa** (the pointed house), thus called due to its cylindrical tower crowned by a green cupola. The **Casa Gispert Saüch**, in Gran Via de Jaume I, and the **Casa Salieti**, in Carrer de la Neu, are also buildings that are well worth a look.

Legends of the city

Girona is a city rich in popular narrative, which, with some basis of original truth and added mythologies gives us an idea of the fears and desires of the old communities. The most famous one has Saint Narcissus, patron saint of Girona, as the leading character, in which he made **giant flies** appear from his uncorrupted body so that their lethal stings would finish off the French invaders. Since the French doggedly persisted in the invasions, popular imagination conveniently adjusted the supposed miracle. The saint also protects against flooding and inflammation of the ear.

The legend of the **petrified witch** tells the typical tale of an old atheist and expert in witchcraft who spent her time swearing and throwing stones at the religious processions. Divine punishment turned her into a stone gargoyle, the only one with human form that can still be seen on one of the buttresses of the cathedral apse. Today the rainwater washes her viperous tongue.

The years of co-existence between Jews and Christians in the Barri Vell also produced tales. They say that before their expulsion, the Hebrews buried their treasure in the Montjüic cemetery, known as **Bou d'Or** (golden ox) in honour of one of the most valuable pieces of the collection. The people of Girona never managed to discover these hidden riches, terrorised by the deafening mooing of the beast that arose from the depths of the earth every time someone dug into the earth with a pick.

The council tourist office periodically organises guided tours of the city. The **legends route** is often the most popular amongst the public. It also organises visits to discover the Jewish legacy, which often includes a culinary tasting session.

The **carrilet**, the little tourist train, is an ideal way of seeing the city for children or those who have difficulty in moving around. Once aboard, tourists are taken through the Barri Vell and part of the new city. The route begins at the Pont de Pedra, lasts around half an hour and provides explanations about the streets and monuments in different languages.

The Virgin of La Pera crowns the stairway

The gargoyle of the witch provoked a myth

The little tourist train leaves from the Pont de Pedra

Cap de Creus shows wild rock formations

Calella de Palafrugell combines beauty with quality tourism

The seabed is a treasure trove in the Islas Medes

The Costa Brava

The Girona coastline between Blanes and Portbou, which goes by the name of the Costa Brava in all the tourist promotional material, does undoubtedly have "brave" areas, such as the precipitous cliff tops of the **Parc Natural del Cap de Creus**, but there are also flat areas such as the **Aiguamolls** (marshlands) **de l'Empordà**, a marvellous natural reserve where birds such as flamingos and storks have taken refuge. The beauty of this stretch of coast is balanced and full of contrasts. Rocky outcrops where the angry waves break make way for the shady pines that sway with the summer siestas. There are still places along the Costa Brava that have been able to resist the battering of cement on the coastline, such as **Llançà, Calella de Palafrugell or Tossa de Mar. Cadaqués**, an artistic and cosmopolitan spot, is also an obligatory visit, despite the winding road. Even more so when the visitor is keenly aware of the unusual concentration of art galleries.

Night owls who follow the discotheque or drinking-hole routes will find what they are looking for without limits in **Lloret de Mar, Platja d'Aro** or **Empúriabrava**. The neo-hippies camp – evidently without paying a penny – in the **Cala Vallpressona**, between Tossa and Santa Cristina de Aro, one of the last libertarian paradises of the Costa Brava, though they should take precautions according to the season, because the very isolation that has conserved the virginity of the spot also brings with it certain risks. The extensive beaches of **Sant Pere Pescador**, often ravaged by the wind, are a paradise for windsurfing enthusiasts. As well as the numerous marine ports and the areas of buoys that ease summertime navigation, there are active fishing ports in **Roses, L'Escala, Palamós and Blanes.**

The Dalí triangle

The **Salvador Dalí Theatre-Museum** in Figueres makes up one of the sides of what has become known as the Dalí Triangle, along with the house in Port Lligat and the castle of Púbol. It is a route that must be taken by all lovers of the art of the genial Figueres painter with the pointed moustache. Even without having some of the great works, the museum gives the visitor an idea of the influence and importance of the Empordà artist in contemporary art. The foundation bearing his name is constantly on the lookout for new works in the international markets. The recent purchase of the lavish collection of jewels exhibited since 2001 in a centre alongside the museum, is a good example of this work. Dalí, who was buried beneath the spectacular geodesic dome that crowns the centre, conceived its surprising surreal touches down to the smallest detail. It should be noted that in the heart of summer long queues form at the entrance and the museum fills up like a tin of sardines. It is time to opt for the evening visit, more refreshing and just as delightful.

One should make the very most of the trip to Figueres by visiting the **Museu del Joguet** (toy) **de Catalunya**, an amazing trip back to the joys of childhood by means of all the gadgets imaginable.

The **house in Port Lligat**, the second side of the Dalí Triangle, is a type of surreal labyrinthine kasbah with incredible decorative elements. The visitor strolls through the splendid garden, which was the setting for wild parties. The **castle of Púbol**, which became the refuge of Gala, the painter's muse, completes the route. Here one can see the surprising sculptures of big-footed elephants.

Inland nature and living stone

A trip inland could start off with a visit to **Banyoles**, where the crossing of the placid waters of the lake in one of the tourist catamarans is de rigor. Another good idea is a relaxing stroll along the lakeside, where a route is marked for walking and cycling. Close to the lake are the **prehistoric caves of Serinyà**, which show the way of life of the first human settlers. Contemporary art lovers must walk through the **wood of Can Ginebreda**, where erotic art and nature have signed a fruitful pact. **Besalú** retains its medieval legacy, as can be seen in the magnificent fortified bridge over the River Fluvià. **Castellfollit de la Roca** provides a spectacular image of its basalt crag with hanging houses. The **volcanic area of la Garrotxa**, with its ancient volcanic cones covered with vegetation, has marvellous green areas such as the **Fageda** (beechwood) **d'en Jordà**, a gigantic wood where you have to be careful not to get lost. In Olot you can visit the Museu dels Volcans (volcanoes). The façade of the church of **Santa Maria de Ripoll** is an authentic "stone Bible" and is considered to be one of the jewels of Catalan Romanesque.

Among the highly interesting monumental remains along the coast feature the Greek and Roman ruins of **Empúries** and the monastery of **Sant Pere de Rodes**, an impressive Romanesque construction that overlooks Port de la Selva. In the **Ripollés** and **Cerdanya** regions, guarding the entrance to the Pyrenees, one can "discover" incredible Romanesque churches in villages that maintain their rural character. The summer greenness, perfect for mountaineering, gives way to the winter snows when skiing is the order of the day.

Routes by car

Unmistakably surrealist touches make the castle of Púbol quite unique

The bridge of Besalú is among the most remarkable of the medieval age

The Fageda d'en Jordà is like an enchanted wood

00

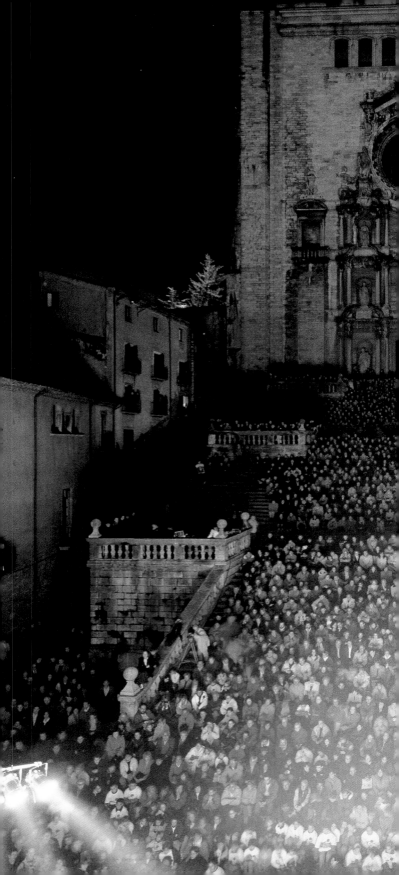

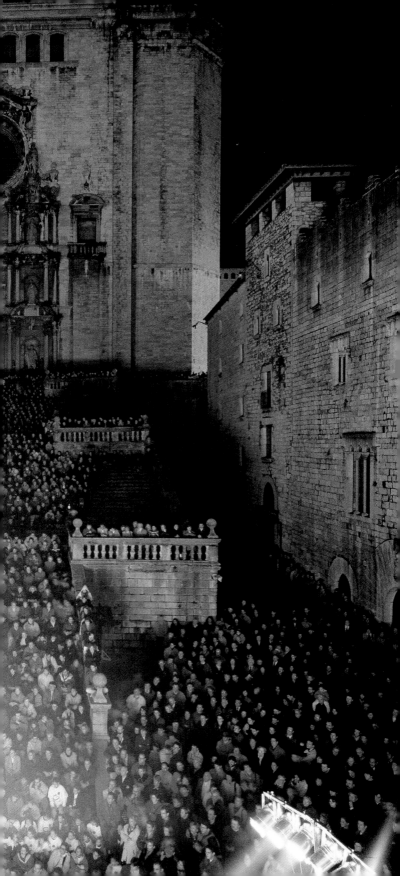

The giants are an essential part of the festivals

Most celebrated days

Fairs of Saint Narcissus
(Between the last weekend of **October** and the first of **November**)
It is the city's annual festival. There are attractions in the Devesa and a commercial fair. Stands and roasted chestnut sellers fill the streets with life. The night-time atmosphere is centred on Passeig de la Copa, where the organisations put up stands and live concerts are held. For more adrenaline-inspired activities you have to enter the Barri Vell under the shower of sparks of the *correfoc* (street parade of firework-laden "devils" with firecrackers, bangers and flares), or watch the human towers of the *castellers* (the participants of the towers) in the Plaça del Vi. The lights and garlands remain in place until Christmas.

Girona flower season
(First fortnight of **May**)
Visitors from all over fill the Barri Vell to enjoy the *temps de flors* (flower season), a sublime fusion of architecture and floriculture. The route enables courtyards and areas not usually accessible to be seen.

Processions and "manaies"
(Good Friday, in **spring**)
The Good Friday procession is led by parade of the *manaies* (literally translated as commanders), a unit of Roman soldiers from the imperial era that impress the public with their gold-plated breastplates and characteristic movements drawing wheels or stars. Following their steps, platforms raised on shoulders with images representing the life and death of Christ. Alongside them march *les vestes* (the tunics), with their heads and bodies hidden beneath long capes and hoods. The climb up to the cathedral of the religious procession is quite spectacular.

Art Fair
(1ˢᵗ of **November**)
At the Art Fair, painters take over the Plaça del Vi and its surrounding area to sell their work directly to the public. An excellent opportunity to acquire art at a good price.

El Tarlà
(**Spring** festivals of the Rambla and on other occasions)
When, centuries gone by, the street was closed for weeks to avoid the Black Death reaching the whole city, a man entertained the bored kids by jumping about on a beam. A popular rag doll (the *tarlà*) now dances as a memory of this event.

The Festival of Saint John
(23ʳᵈ of **June**)
During the shortest night of the year bonfires are lit, made from all the household junk, a custom in villages and cities in Catalan-speaking lands. After the fires come the dancing, firecrackers, cava and cake.

Christmas
The ancient tradition of *cagar el tió* lives on. For a week the children have been "feeding" the *tió* (log) and now they sing a song and hit it with a stick to make it (and here we translate literally and bluntly) crap the presents they are hoping for. In the nativity scenes that reproduce the birth of Jesus, a *caganer* (crapper) is often placed, giving them an anti-clerical touch.

Parade of the Three Kings of the Orient
(5ᵗʰ of **January**)
In Girona, before going through the streets in a brightly-lit parade, the Three Kings of the Orient camp next to the city walls, where the children give them their last-minute letters containing the list of presents they have asked for.

Artists sell their work personally

Culture

Festivals and other cultural events

Festival of world religious music. First week of July.

Jazz Festival of Girona. 2nd fortnight of September.

El Pati (The courtyard). International festival of amateur theatre, biennial in even years. A week during September.

Record Collectors Fair. First weekend in March, Fira de Girona.

Temporada Alta (High Season). International theatre festival. From October to November. Teatre Municipal, Sala La Planeta and Teatre de Salt.

Festival of Cinema of Girona. Devoted to short films. One week in September. Casa de Cultura and cinemas across the city.

El dret a la mirada (The right to look). Biennial. Exhibition of photography and other image related arts. In autumn. Different venues in the city.

Catalan book week. February. Casa de la Cultura.

Cinemas

Truffaut. Original language version. Film library, Late night sessions and children's films at the weekend. C/Portal Nou, 7 (Barri Vell). Tel. 972 22 50 44

Òscar. 11 screens. Late night sessions. Sant Ponç leisure area, (north exit). Tel. 972 20 71 52

Lauren. 9 screens. Late night sessions. Polígono Mas Xirgu leisure area (south exit). Tel. 972 23 05 16

Albéniz. 10 screens. Late night sessions. C/ Jeroni Real de Fontclara, 2-4 (Plaça Independència area). Tel. 972 41 01 10

Albéniz Plaça. 3 screens. Plaça Jordi de Sant Jordi, 1. Tel. 972 41 06 60

Theatres

Teatre Municipal. Plaça del Vi, 1. Tel. 972 41 90 10

Sala La Planeta. Passeig Canalejas, 6. Tel. 972 22 77 19

Auditori de La Mercè. Pujada de la Mercè, 12 Tel. 972 22 33 05

Teatre de Salt. In Salt. Metropolitan programme. Plaça Sant Jaume. Tel. 972 40 20 04

Cultural centres

Casa de Cultura de Girona. Library, exhibitions, concerts, courses, conferences, theatre workshop, etc. Plaça de l'Hospital, 6. Tel. 972 20 20 13

La Mercè. Exhibitions, auditorium, courses, conferences, art school, etc. Pujada de la Mercè, 12. Tel. 972 22 33 05

Exhibition centres

Centre Cultural Caixa de Girona-Fontana d'Or. Several rooms. C/ Ciutadans, 19. Tel. 972 18 22 29

Col·legi d'Arquitectes. Pl. de la Catedral, 8. Tel. 972 41 27 27

Espais. Contemporary Art Centre. C/ Pou Rodó, 5-7 Tel. 972 20 25 30

Sales Municipals d'Exposició. Rambla, 1. Tel. 972 22 33 05

Sala Girona de "la Caixa". Popular and informative exhibitions. C/ Sèquia, 5. Tel. 972 21 84 79

Sant Nicolau. Contemporary art exhibitions. C/ Santa Llúcia, 1. Tel. 972 41 20 63

Art Galleries

Artnau. C/ Santa Clara, 60. Tel. 972 20 68 64
Can Marc. C/ de la Força, 13. Tel. 972 21 89 58
El Claustre. C/ Nou, 8-9-10. Tel. 972 20 31 26
Expoart. C/ Hortes, 22b. Tel. 972 21 64 65
Expocambra. C/ Ciutadans, 12. Tel. 972 20 06 16
Marcart. C/ Perill, 3. Tel. 972 21 82 40
Palau de Caramany. Pujada de Sant Domènec, 1. Tel. 972 21 35 64
Palau de la Mercè. Pujada de la Mercè, 10. Tel. 972 22 41 30

Civic centres

Sant Narcís. Plaça Assumpció, 27. Tel. 972 23 70 63
Onyar. C/ Camp de la Plana, 13. Tel. 972 20 89 55
Pont Major. C/ Sant Joan Bosco, 122. Tel. 972 20 52 44
Pedret. C/ de Pedret, 152-156, bajos. Tel. 972 20 52 44
Santa Eugènia. C/ Santa Eugènia, 124. Tel. 972 24 51 11

Archives and libraries

Public Library. Plaça de l'Hospital, 6. Tel. 972 20 22 52
Historic Archive of the City. Plaça de l'Institut vell, 1. Tel. 972 22 15 45
Historical Archive of Girona. Plaça de Sant Josep, 1. Tel. 972 21 80 12
Taialà Municipal Library. Ctra. Taialà, 75. Tel. 972 21 33 15
Salvador Allende Municipal Library. C/, Montseny, 74-78. Tel. 972 23 27 15

Schools

Modern Music and Jazz School. C/ Santa Eugènia, 124. Tel. 972 23 69 79
Municipal School of Fine Arts. Pujada de la Mercè, 12. Tel. 972 22 33 05
El Galliner Theatre School. Children and adults. Plaça de l'Hospital, 6. Tel. 972 20 58 84

Dervishes in the Religious Music Festival

THE HANDICRAFT SHOPS SELLING PRODUCTS MADE IN THE WORKSHOP AT THE BACK WITH CARE AND DEVOTION ARE A DYING BREED. THE MAJORITY OF CRAFTSMEN AND WOMEN OF THE CITY HAVE BEEN FORCED TO CLOSE DOWN, SQUEEZED OUT BY THE IMPERATIVES OF PRODUCTIVITY IN THESE NEW TIMES. NEVERTHELESS, THERE ARE STILL ARTISANS AND REPRESENTATIVES OF OLD TRADES WHO PRACTICE THEIR ARCHAIC ACTIVITIES AS A HOBBY AND, ONCE A WEEK, OFFER THEIR PRODUCTS IN HANDICRAFT FAIRS.

Some artisans help maintain the old traditions

Pont de Pedra Handicraft Fair. Every Saturday on the Pont de Pedra, the Association of Artisans of Girona organises a handicrafts fair that enables the best manufacturers from the city and outlying villages to display and sell their products on a rotary basis. The system for occupying the canvas stands installed over the cobblestones of the bridge provides an ever-changing spectacle of curious and handcrafted objects.

Association of Artisans of Girona. Among its members, subject to controls that guarantee the authenticity of their manual work, there are basket makers, tinsmiths, flower arrangers, potters, leather and silver workers, lacemakers... To contact them: Alfons Hernández, calle Rutlla, 22. Tel. 972 38 90 64

Ferros d'Art Cadenas. This shop, which sells cast iron lamps and other metal utensils forms one of the few examples of the old artisan system, that made manufacturing and selling two compatible activities. Part of the space, facing the more commercial part of the street, is a stunning and packed showroom of lamps, but by entering through a long corridor, the customer enters the darkness of the workshop, where the crude metals are hammered into shape. C/ Nou, 5. Tel. 972 20 26 72

Ramon Boix. Everything in copper and brass utensils. His hands have produced the armour worn by the *manaies* during Easter. C/ Ballesteries, 17. Tel. 972 20 67 97

Sweet handicrafts

THE LOCAL STAR IS THE *XUIXO* (DOUGHNUT) FILLED WITH CUS-
TARD AND COVERED IN SUGAR, SUPPOSEDLY INVENTED AT THE
BEGINNING OF THE 20TH CENTURY FROM A CAKE OF FRENCH
ORIGIN. A GLANCE AT THE WINDOWS OF THE GIRONA PATIS-
SERIES IS A REMINDER THAT EVEN THOSE WITH THE SWEETEST
TOOTH WOULD HAVE TROUBLE POLISHING OFF EVERYTHING
THEY OFFER.

Castelló Cake Shop. A good spot to get the traditional
Girona *xuixo*. Also highly recommended are the *panellets*
(marzipan and almond) and *brunyols* (fritters). C/ Santa
Clara, 45. Tel. 972 20 32 81

Faure Cake Shop. Figures of popular characters made in
chocolate and other sweet novelties. C/ Argenteria, 25.
Tel. 972 20 17 87

La Vienesa Cake Shop. A patisserie where you can eat
with your eyes. You must choose the speciality and then sit
down and enjoy it slowly. Pujada del Pont de Pedra, 1.
Tel. 972 48 60 46

Roca Cake Shop. Specialists in *bombons de músic*, chocolates with nuts and raisins. C/ Migdia, 17.
Tel. 972 20 98 82

Tornés Cake Shop. One of the most famous shops in the
enlarged district. Travessia de la Creu, 25.
Tel. 972 20 74 33

Turrons Candela. The only two places where you will find
the famous and much-loved *turrons* (traditional candies) of
"Victoriano Candela e hijos", where, moreover, the taste of
the *orxata* (cold drink made from tiger nuts and almonds)
has not been watered down. C/ Sant Anselm Clavé, 3, tel.
972 21 11 03 and c/ Argenteria, 8. tel. 972 22 09 38

Gluki Chocolates Shop. Since 1880, this company from
Olot has produced marvellous chocolates made from Central American cocoa. Their additive-free chocolates are
excellent. C/ Argenteria, 26. Tel. 972 20 19 89

The "xuixo" is the best-known local pastry

Gastronomy

GIRONA HAS NEVER BEEN ABLE TO BOAST OF BEING THE GAS-
TRONOMIC CAPITAL OF THE REGION, BUT IN RECENT YEARS IT
HAS BEEN ABLE TO RAISE ITS LEVEL IN TERMS OF QUALITY. THE
INFLUENCE OF NEARBY CUISINE OF GREAT FAME, SUCH AS
THAT OF EMPORDÀ, AND THE DECISION OF SOME RESTAU-
RANTS TO INNOVATE HAS MADE GIRONA AN ESSENTIAL PORT
OF CALL FOR THE MOST DEMANDING GASTRONOMES. DESPITE
THE FACT THAT THE LEVEL OF THE POPULAR RESTAURANTS IS
DISCREET, THERE ARE A GOOD NUMBER OF ESTABLISHMENTS
WHERE THE SO-CALLED MARKET CUISINE RESULTS IN EXQUIS-
ITE MEALS BEING PRODUCED FROM PRODUCTS BOUGHT DAILY
FROM THE LLEÓ MUNICIPAL MARKET. THE SMALL PLOTS AND
FARMS OF THE AREA ARE A GUARANTEE OF FINE PRODUCE.
ONE OUTSTANDING LOCAL DELICACY IS THE *BOTIFARRA DOLÇA*,
CURED SAUSAGE THAT MIXES MINCEMEAT WITH SUGAR AND
WHICH HAS THOSE WITH A SWEET TOOTH LICKING THEIR LIPS.

For more refined palates

El celler de Can Roca. For demanding gastronomes, the
best of the city. Awarded with two stars in the Michelin
Guide. High quality creative cuisine. The in-season taster
menu is recommendable. 30-45 €. Ctra. Taialà, 40.
Tel. 972 22 21 57

Massana. Exquisitely prepared traditional and market cuisine. 30-35 €. C/ Bonastruc ça Porta, 10. Tel. 972 21 38 20

Albereda. Home-made Catalan and market cuisine.
Menu of *carpaccios* and kid filled with *butifarra* (sausage).
25-35 €. C/ Albereda, 9. Tel. 972 22 60 02

Restaurant de l'Escola d'Hostaleria. The restaurateurs of
the future show off their talent and prepare succulent
made-to-order menus. Open lunchtime during the week.
15-25 €. C/ Josep Viader, 11. Tel. 972 22 01 22

El Pati Verd. Mediterranean cuisine. The most prestigious
hotel restaurant in the city prepares dishes with foie gras,
carpaccios and filets. 30-35 €. Plaça Miquel Santaló, 10.
Tel. 972 21 12 12

La Penyora. Market cuisine and art in the heart of the
Barri Vell. 20-25€. C/ Nou del Teatre, 3. Tel. 972 21 89 48

Cal Ros. Home-made Catalan cuisine. Veal fricassée and
arròs negre (rice with squid ink). 18-20 €. C/ Cort Reial, 9.
Tel. 972 21 73 79

Gastronomy

Affordable meals for all

Àpats. Market cuisine with a daily menu. 12 €. Av. Jaume I, 22. Tel. 972 21 84 31

Boira. Catalan and market cuisine. Excellent view of the houses on the Onyar. 18-20 €. Plaça Independència, 17. Tel. 972 20 30 96

Ca l'Àvia. Grilled meat. Kitchen open until 2 in the morning. 12-18 €. C/ Porvenir, 10 (west exit). Tel. 972 21 11 22

Bar Cadillac Cafè. Mediterranean cuisine. Open until 2.20 a.m. Pub atmosphere. 12-18 €. Ctra. Barcelona, 130 (southern exit of the city). Tel. 972 22 84 52

Bronsom's. Catalan and market cuisine. Fish *suquet* (soup) and *arròs negre* (rice with squid ink). 12 €. Av. Sant Francesc, 7. Tel. 972 21 24 93

Ca l'Ivan. Catalan and market cuisine. 12-15 €. Ronda Ferran Puig, 1-3. Tel. 972 20 14 30

Ca la Pilar. Catalan and market cuisine. 17 €. C/ Pont Major, 124 (north exit). Tel. 972 21 28 61

Can Lloret. Traditional cuisine and daily set menu. Views over the Onyar. 12-15 €. Plaça de la Independència, 14. Tel. 972 21 36 71

Can Marquès. Home-made and market cuisine. 18-25 €. Plaça Calvet i Rubalcaba, 3. Tel. 972 20 10 01

Can Peret. Market cuisine. 18-15 €. C/ Sacsimort, 6 (Barri Vell). Tel. 972 21 39 68

Casa Marieta. Traditional cuisine. Spacious hundred-year-old redecorated restaurant. Open daily from lunchtime to night. 15-20 €. Plaça Independència, 5-6. Tel. 972 20 10 16

Cipresaia. Mediterranean and home-made cuisine. 15-18 €. C/ General Fournàs, 2 (Barri Vell). Tel. 972 22 24 49

Edelweiss. Market cuisine. One of the best wine lists in the city. 18-20 €. Passatge Ensesa in Carrer de Santa Eugènia, 7 (west exit). Tel. 972 20 18 97

A painstakingly crafted plate, produced in El Celler de Can Roca

El Museu del Vi. Bar meals. Set menus. 8-12 €. C/ Cort Reial, 4 (Barri Vell). Tel. 972 21 34 85

Els Cairats. Market cuisine. 10-15 €. C/ Cardenal Margarit, 6. Tel. 972 21 14 01

El Pati Blau. Home-made Catalan cuisine. Value for money select menus. *Farcellets* (stuffed) pigs trotters and veal cheek *civet* (stew). 10-20 €. C/ Lorenzana, 15. Tel. 972 22 42 99

El 21 de Josep Pla. Varied daily menus. 10-12 €. Plaça Josep Pla (Mercadal district). Tel. 972 20 21 31

La Fundició. Market cuisine. 10-15 €. C/ Maluquer Salvador, 30 (enlarged district). Tel. 972 48 56 33

L'Argadà. Catalan cuisine and excellent cured meats. 10-15 €. C/ Ramon Folch, 7. Tel. 972 21 84 05

La Columna. Market cuisine. 10-15 €. C/ de Baix, 40 (towards Salt). Tel. 972 24 41 35

La Churraskita. Argentine cuisine. All kinds of meat dishes. 10-15 €. C/ Pedret, 101 (Pedret district). Tel. 972 20 95 14

La Llarga. Creative market cuisine. 18-20 €. Av. Sant Francesc, 11. Tel. 972 20 10 18

Nelson. Catalan cuisine. Affordable menus. 10-15 €. C/ Lorenzana, 44 (enlarged district). Tel. 972 21 26 18

El Palau de la Mercè. Creative and market cuisine. Beautiful courtyard at the foot of the wall. C/ Beates s/n (Barri Vell). Tel. 972 22 80 14

Pizzeria Café Mozart. Market cuisine and pizzas. 10-15 €. Plaça Independència, 2. Tel. 972 20 75 42

Pizzeries El Racó. Mediterranean cuisine. Pasta, pizzas, crêpes and meat dishes. 10-15 €. C/ Santa Clara, 47 and C/ Maluquer Salvador, 9. Tel. 972 22 16 89

Llegendes. Mediterranean cuisine and fresh fish dishes. 15-20 €. C/ Riera Can Camaret, 3 (Pont Major). Tel. 972 22 07 09

Marisquería Rías Gallegas. Fresh fish, sea cucumbers and brown crabs. 15-30 €. Av. Lluís Pericot, 74 (Palau district). Tel. 972 21 94 34

Til·la. Vegetarian. Vegetable cannelloni and vegetarian taster menu. 10-15 €. Av. Sant Narcís, 65 (Sant Narcís district). Tel. 972 23 45 45

Pol Nord. Creative cuisine. Warm prawn and mushroom salad. 15-25 €. C/ Pedret, 120. Tel. 972 20 09 27

Sifó Café. Catalan cuisine and grilled. 10-12 €. Ronda Ferran Puig, 39 (Devesa area). Tel. 972 48 52 70

International cuisine

Downtown. American cuisine. Crispy chicken and entrecôte steaks. 10-12 €. C/ Santa Eugènia, 11. Tel. 972 21 87 65

El cul de la lleona. Moroccan dishes and desserts. Couscous and dips. 15-19 €. C/ Calderers, 8 (Barri Vell). Tel. 972 20 31 58

Primo Piatto. Italian cuisine. Home-made tagliolini and tiramisu. 20-25 €. C/ Pedret, 136. Tel. 972 22 35 21

El Balcó. Argentine cuisine. Meat roulade and steaks. 20-24 €. C/ Hortes, 16. Tel. 972 22 31 61

La Crepêrie Bretonne. Spécialistés bretonnes. Breton specialities. Saracen wheat pie and Normandy crêpes. 10-15 €. C/ Cort Reial, 14. Tel. 972 21 81 20

Lagunak. Basque-Navarra cuisine. Seafood and Donosti-style ox. 25-30 €. C/ Pedret, 136. Tel. 972 41 22 91

Taco-taco. Mexican and Tex-Mex cuisine. 12-15 €. C/ Nord, 22. Tel. 972 22 21 04

Gran Muralla. Chinese cuisine. Beijing duck and prawns with mushrooms. 10-12 €. C/ Eiximenis, 15. Tel. 972 22 23 47

Asador de La Barca. Castilian cuisine. Suckling pork and Burgos-style lamb. 25-35 €. C/ Pont de la Barca, 1. Tel. 972 20 42 23

Some restaurants satisfy both the palate and the eyesight

Cafés/evening drinks

The people of Girona have the benefit of an enhanced supply of diverse and comfortable public houses and bars, suitable for chatting, wild partying or seduction. The nightlife starts taking off from Thursday – when the university students get raving – and keeps going till Saturday.

Cafés

L'Antiga. Breakfasts and teas. Their *xocolata desfeta* (hot melted chocolate) is unforgettable. Plaça del Vi, 8. Tel. 972 21 66 81

Bar Núria. Many night-time soirees end here in the early hours, on its glass isle amidst the cars. Opens early Plaça Poeta Marquina, s/n. Tel. 972 20 30 76

Boira. Big terrace for eating alfresco in summer and a warm inside with big windows overlooking the houses on the Onyar. C/ Santa Clara, 60. Tel. 972 20 54 84

Granja Mora. Small café that preserves a part of the city's history. C/ Cort Reial, 18. Tel. 972 20 22 38

L'Arc. It was a focal point for the anti-Franco struggle. It boasts of a cathedral in the courtyard. The terrace is the ideal spot to take in the city's most imposing building. Plaça de la Catedral, 9. Tel. 972 20 30 87

La Boireta. Ideal for going with restless children since its terrace backs on to the park. Parc Central.

Campus. Student atmosphere. Next to the University of Girona. Plaça de Sant Domènec, 1. Tel. 972 22 44 76

La Llibreria. Bookshop and cafeteria, this café holds meetings and presentations. C/ Ciutadans, 15. Tel. 972 20 48 18

La Terra. Windows overlooking the river. Excellent sandwiches. C/ Ballesteries, 23. Tel. 972 21 57 64

Le Bistrot. Classical café in "retro" style. In summer, its tables occupy one of the most beautiful spots in the Barri Vell. The menus and "country" pizzas are recommended. Pujada de Sant Domènec. Tel. 972 21 88 03

Los Padules. One of the last corners of what was in its day the *carrer dels torrats* (the drunks' street) as it was

The afternoon chat is still encouraged at the Doble Set cafe

baptised by a local rock group. Snacks and wines. C/ Nou del Teatre, 10. Tel. 972 20 30 54

Royal. Large choice of beers and fruit juices. Plaça de la Independència, 1. Tel. 972 22 42 62

Evening drinks

Aleshores. Central pub with a very diverse public. Plaça de la Independència, 4. Tel. 972 22 06 06

Nummulit. One of the night spots with the most history. Frequented by journalists, literati and other night birds. C/ Nord, 7-9. Tel. 972 41 04 05

La Via. This is amongst the most successful spots in the Pedret night-time area, which has the highest concentration of bars per square metre in the city. C/ Pedret, 66. Tel. 972 41 04 61

Sidharta. Cocktails and select drinks. C/ Pedret, 116.

Fractal. The bar that represents the night-time atmosphere of the enlarged district. In the afternoons, games of *botifarra* (popular card game) and in the evening, a packed music bar. C/ Maluquer Salvador, 5. Tel. 972 21 82 35

Discotheques, pubs and dance balls

Local & Bar Platea. The big night-time temple. An old theatre reconverted by the magic of bold design. Blues and soul performances on Wednesdays. C/ Jeroni Real de Fontclara, 4. Tel. 972 22 72 88

La Sala del Cel. Avant-garde technodiscotheque, famed across Europe. The best DJs. C/ Pedret, 118. Tel. 972 21 46 64

7è Art. On of the few "classical" discotheques in the city. Mas Xirgu leisure area. Tel. 972 23 73 25

La Sala de Ball. Classical dancing with live orchestras at weekends and on public holidays. Thursday nights, student bashes. Passeig de la Devesa. Tel. 972 20 28 89

Marquees of the Devesa. In summer, the night owls look for the cool of the Devesa Park. Open June to September.

Terrace in the Plaça Poeta Marquina

Carrer Ballesteries is the gift shop centre

THERE ARE AN EXTRAORDINARY AMOUNT OF GOODS ON OFFER AND BOTH THE RESIDENTS OF GIRONA AND THE NEARBY TOWNS FREQUENTLY SHOP IN THE STREETS OF THE CENTRE OR THE ENLARGED DISTRICT. IT IS ESTIMATED THAT SOME 40% OF THE SHOPS IN THE CITY CENTRE SELL CLOTHES OR COMPLEMENTS. THE MAJORITY OF THESE SHOPS ARE CENTRED IN CARRER (STREET) NOU AND CARRER SANTA CLARA, AND IN THE RAMBLA, ALTHOUGH WORTH MENTIONING IS THE RISING LEVEL OF COMMERCIAL ACTIVITY IN CARRER BALLESTERIES, A GOOD SPOT FOR BUYING SMALL GIFTS OR SOUVENIRS. WITHOUT AIMING TO PROVIDE AN EXHAUSTIVE LIST, WE CAN RECOMMEND THE FOLLOWING SHOPS:

Amsterdam. Underground clothes. C/ Ballesteries, 4.

Art Musical Grabulosa. Instruments and musical accessories. Plaça del Oli, 1. Tel. 972 20 29 11

Bona Pasta. Fresh home-made pasta and take-away dishes. C/ Ballesteries, 12. Tel. 972 21 16 29

Can Ventura. Select take-away. For demanding palates. C/ Nou, 7. Tel. 972 20 00 24

Carnisseria Can Juandó. Centrally located, for buying the celebrated Girona veal and top quality cured meats. C/ Nou, 23. Tel. 972 20 27 42

Eco-Opció. Organic and natural products. C/ Ballesteries, 50. Tel. 972 41 13 73

El celler d'en Pere. Small wine cellar where you can buy excellent wine. C/ Bonaventura Carreras i Peralta, 2. Tel. 972 21 22 88

Floristeria Freesia Interflora. Variety of flowers and plants. C/ Antoni Maria Claret, 10, and 15-29. Tel. 972 20 58 10

Fusteria Joan Nierga. A small shop where anything made of wood rules here. C/ Albereda, 1. Tel. 972 20 54 22

Harmonia Mundi. World music. C/ Cort Reial, 21. Tel. 972 20 62 65

Karla. Candles and wax. Useful for decoration and DIY. C/ Ballesteries, 21-22. Tel. 972 20 59 14

Carrer Argenteria still houses some jewellery shops

La Carpa. Toys and all kinds of small and original gadgets for gifts. C/ Ballesteries, 37. Tel. 972 21 20 02

La Moda. An institution in the sale of cotton threads and balls of wool. Plaça del Vi, 13. Tel. 972 20 20 95

La Rellotgeria. Repair, restoration and sale of old watches and clocks. C/ Ballesteries, 45. Tel. 972 21 69 19

Lubna. Imported fashion, footwear and records. C/ Mercaders, 24. Tel. 972 20 44 89

Llibreria Geli. The best book collection in the city. Company established over one hundred years. C/ Argenteria, 18. Tel. 972 20 17 90

Llibreria 22. Bookshop with presentations of books and meeting point for Girona authors. C/ Hortes, 22. Tel. 972 21 23 95

Moby Disk. Independent music. Plaça del Vi, 4.

Moriscot. Cured meats and select products. With an unbeatable wine cellar. A paradise for epicures. C/ Ciutadans, 4. Tel. 972 20 09 58

Nyigui-Nyogui. One of the veteran shops in the sale of original gifts. C/ Mercaders, 12.

Portal del Col·leccionista. Selling and buying of old books, engravings and postcards. Surprising relics. C/ de la Força, 25. Tel. 972 21 55 69

Puig Ferreteria. From the hammer to the anvil. Rambla, 22. Tel. 972 20 02 48

Recorda-t'en. Souvenirs of the city. Handicrafts and traditions. C/ Calderers, 12. Tel. 972 22 78 90

Samarkanda. Exotic wooden furniture. Plaça del Oli, 2. Tel. 972 41 11 64

Sant Fèlix. Souvenirs of the city. Handicrafts and traditions. C/ Calderers, 10. Tel. 972 20 43 88

Souvenirs AD Records. Pujada Sant Feliu, 5. Tel. 972 21 88 06

Tatto. Artistic tattoos. C/ Mercaders, 22.

Ulysus. Bookshop specialising in travel, maps and travel books. C/ Ballesteries, 29. Tel. 972 21 17 73

Accommodation

There are not that many hotels, especially in the centre of the city. This means that at certain times of the year it can be quite difficult to find the type of desired accommodation, although there is always the possibility of finding a hotel room in the outlying towns.

Hotels

**** **Carlemany.** The most central and modern. This is the hotel for executives and VIP guests. Bar, restaurant, piano-bar open until the early hours, meeting rooms, car park, etc. Approximate price for double room: 115 €. Plaça Miquel Santaló (in the enlarged district). Tel. 972 21 12 12. Internet: www.carlemany. es.

**** **Melià Confort.** The second big hotel in the city. Bar, restaurant, meeting rooms, car park, etc. Dogs accepted. Approximate price for double room: 114 €. Ctra. de Barcelona, 112 (south exit). Tel. 972 40 05 00

*** **Costabella.** A top-class hotel although it is on the outskirts. Bar, restaurant, garden, meeting rooms, car park, etc. Dogs accepted. Approximate price for double room: 109 €. Av. de França, 61 (north exit). Tel. 972 20 25 24

*** **Ultònia.** The most central large hotel. Bar, meeting rooms, etc. Approximate price for double room: 77 €. Gran Via de Jaume I, 22. Tel. 972 20 38 50

** **Europa.** A small hotel, without big luxuries, but managed with great professionalism. Bar. Approximate price for double room: 55 €. C/ Juli Garreta, 21 (enlarged district)). Tel. 972 20 27 50

* **Condal.** Dogs accepted. Approximate price for double room: 44 €. C/ Joan Maragall, 10. Tel. 972 20 44 62

* **Peninsular.** Old but very central. Approximate price for double room: 56 €. C/ Nou, 3. Tel. 972 20 38 00

The Hotel Carlemany opens up to a busy square

The old part of Girona has hardly any accommodation facilities

Pensions and other accommodation

** **Bellmirall.** Family pension in the heart of the Barri Vell. Only 7 rooms. Approximate price for double room: 39 €. C/ Bellmirall, 3. Tel. 972 20 40 09

* **Margarit**. Approximate price for double room: 29 €. C/ Ultònia, 1. Tel. 972 20 10 66

* **Barnet.** Very central. Daily menu. Approximate price for double room: 23 €. C/ Santa Clara, 16. Tel. 972 20 00 33

* **Mercedes.** Approximate price for double room: 22 €. Ctra. de Barcelona, 99. Tel. 972 20 30 28

* **Alhambra.** Approximate price for double room: 30 €. C/ Bassegoda, 18. Tel. 972 23 29 03

* **Borràs.** Approximate price for double room: 25 €. Travessera Auriga, 6. Tel. 972 22 40 08

* **Can Rafel.** Approximate price for double room: 20 €. Ctra. de Barcelona, 85. Tel. 972 21 40 78

* **Coll.** Daily menu. Approximate price for double room: 30 €. C/ Hortes, 24. Tel. 972 20 30 86

* **Hostal Gerunda.** Approximate price for double room: 29 €. Ctra. Barcelona, 34. Tel. 972 20 22 85

* **Lladó.** Approximate price for double room: 24 €. C/ La Barca, 31.Tel. 972 21 09 98

Apartaments Històric Barri Vell. Approximate price: 30 €. C/ Bellmirall, 4. Tel. 972 22 35 83

Youth Hostel. Forms part of the network of youth hostels of the Generalitat. Freely available places in summer. Very affordable restaurant. C/ Ciutadans, 9. Tel. 972 21 80 03

Camping Can Toni Manescal. Ctra. de Llambilles, km. 2. Fornells de la Selva. Open all year. Swimming pool. Price per pitch, car, tent and light: 9 €. Tel. 972 47 61 17

Services

Tourist information

Pick-up point	972 21 16 78
Tourist Office La Rambla	972 22 65 75
Citizens information bureau	972 41 90 10
Tourism of the Generalitat	972 20 33 50
Costa Brava Tourist Board	972 20 84 01

Emergencies

Red Cross ambulances	112 / 972 22 22 22
Fire Service	085 / 972 18 24 00
Mossos d'Esquadra (Catalan Police)	088 / 972 21 34 50
Crime victims attention	972 21 90 60
Local Police	092 / 972 41 90 92
National Police	091 / 972 20 50 50
Civil Guard	062
Civil Protection	972 41 86 55
Emergencies	112
Maritime emergencies	900 20 22 02

Medical and healthcare centres

Hospital Josep Trueta	972 20 27 00
Hospital Santa Caterina	972 18 26 00
Psychiatric Hospital	972 18 25 00
Güell Clinic (specialities)	972 21 87 80
First Aid Centre	972 20 00 12
Clínica Girona	972 20 45 00
Clínica L'Aliança	972 20 48 81
Clínica Bofill	972 20 43 50
Medical Diagnosis Bureau	972 20 48 82

Transport and communication

Renfe (train)	972 24 02 02
Girona-Costa Brava Airport	972 18 66 00
Bus Station	972 21 23 19
Iberia (airline company)	902 40 05 00
Transmediterránea (ferry company)	902 45 46 45
Local buses	972 20 48 68
Taxis	972 22 10 20
Taxis (for the disabled)	972 22 23 23
Vehicle Inspection Centre	972 49 28 88

Car hire

Avis	972 20 69 33
Atesa	972 22 15 52
Cabeza	972 21 82 08
Europ Car	972 20 99 46
Hertz	972 41 00 68
Marius	972 22 09 06

| New Car | 972 20 32 86 |
| Tot Auto | 972 47 64 06 |

Intercity buses

Sarfa
Daily services to the Costa Brava,
Barcelona, Figueres; national
and international routes — 972 30 06 23
Teisa
Daily services to the Garrotxa — 972 57 00 53
Barcelona Bus
Daily services to Barcelona, Blanes,
Tordera and Figueres — 972 20 24 32
Rafael Mas
Services to Lloret de Mar — 972 36 40 72
La Hispano Hilariense
Services to Salt, Arbúcies and Sant Hilari — 972 23 79 54
Ampsa
Serv. to Torroella de Montgrí and l'Estartit — 972 21 63 53

Institutions, official bodies and others

City Council	972 41 90 00
Generalitat (attention to public)	012
Girona Provincial Council	972 18 50 00
Sub-delegation of the Government	972 41 86 00
Courts (attention to public)	972 18 17 00
Post Office	972 20 32 36
Defence Delegation	972 20 01 28
Catalan Traffic Service	972 41 32 00
University of Girona	972 41 80 00
Fira de Girona trade fair centre	972 41 91 00

Other numbers of interest

National directory enquiries	11818
International directory enquiries	025
Water (local water board)	972 20 17 37
Electricity (Fecsa-Endesa company)	900 70 70 70
	900 77 07 77
Gas (Gas Natural)	900 75 07 50
	900 76 07 60
Bishopric of Girona	972 41 28 84
Bar Association	972 21 02 08
NGO Solidarity Committee	972 21 99 16
Emergency veterinary services	972 21 86 68
Meteorological information	906 36 53 65
Consumer Rights Office	972 41 90 10
Pavelló Mun. de Palau (swimming pool)	972 22 21 55
Municipal Swimming Pools of Devesa	972 20 93 54
GEiEG (sports club)	972 20 29 46

Services

Media

TV3	972 20 20 26
TVE	972 21 98 73
Local Girona TV	972 22 11 11
Diari de Girona	972 20 20 66
El Punt	972 18 64 00
Catalunya Ràdio	972 21 37 38
RNE	972 41 60 60

Telephone and Communication companies

Movistar	1485
Moviline	1485
Airtel	1444
Aló	1428
Amena	1474
American Telecom	1582
BT Comunicaciones	1433
Jazztel	1433
Menta (Cable in Girona)	900 70 05 00
Retevision	015
Uni2	1414

Cancelling credit and bank cards

4b (Master Card, Visa...)	913 62 62 00
American Express	915 72 03 03
Red 6.000	915 96 53 35
Sevi Red (Master Card, Visa...)	915 19 21 00

Prefixes for making calls abroad

00 + the country code + the city code (if necessary) + number of person you are calling. Some prefix codes for different countries:

Germany	49
Andorre (without city code)	376
United States	1
France (without city code)	33
Ireland (without city code)	354
Italy	39
United Kingdom	44

Internet addresses with information links

www.ajuntament.gi
www.ddgi.es
www.girona.com
www.gironahoy.com
www.gencat.es